Cooking with Nonna

Dona Herweck Rice

Publishing Credits

Rachelle Cracchiolo, M.S.Ed., *Publisher*
Conni Medina, M.A.Ed., *Managing Editor*
Nika Fabienke, Ed.D., *Content Director*
Véronique Bos, *Creative Director*
Shaun N. Bernadou, *Art Director*
Valerie Morales, *Associate Editor*
John Leach, *Assistant Editor*
Courtney Roberson, *Senior Graphic Designer*

Image Credits: All images from iStock and/or Shutterstock.

Library of Congress Cataloging-in-Publication Data

Names: Rice, Dona, author.
Title: Cooking with Nonna / Dona Herweck Rice.
Description: Huntington Beach, CA : Teacher Created Materials, [2019] | Identifiers: LCCN 2018029706 (print) | LCCN 2018031704 (ebook) | ISBN 9781493899203 | ISBN 9781493898466
Subjects: LCSH: Cooking, Italian--Juvenile literature. | LCGFT: Cookbooks.
Classification: LCC TX723 (ebook) | LCC TX723 .R485 2019 (print) | DDC 641.5945--dc23
LC record available at https://lccn.loc.gov/2018029706

Teacher Created Materials
5301 Oceanus Drive
Huntington Beach, CA 92649-1030
www.tcmpub.com
ISBN 978-1-4938-9846-6
© 2019 Teacher Created Materials, Inc.
Printed in China
Nordica.082018.CA21800936

She made two ,

meatballs

and I made more.

 the  .

Count   meatballs

What is the number?

3

She made two ,
pizzas

and I made more.

 the pizzas.

Count

What is the number?

She made two ,
buns

and I made more.

Count   buns

What is the number?

She made two ,
salads

and I made more.

 the salads.

Count

What is the number?

She made two ,
cookies

and I made more.

What is the number?

Count  the cookies.

High-Frequency New Words

Review Words

is
and
two
number
made

New Words

the
I
what
she
more